Mary and Martha's Dinner Guest

Luke 10:38–42 for children

Written by Swanee Ballman

Illustrated by Joe Boddy

Arch® Books
Copyright © 1998 Concordia Publishing House
3558 S. Jefferson Avenue, St. Louis, MO 63118-3968
Manufactured in the United States of America

In a suburb of Jerusalem—
In a town called Bethany—
Lived two sisters who loved Jesus
Named Martha and Mary.

The Lord and His disciples
Had walked for many a mile.
When they got to Martha's house,
They decided to stay awhile.

Jesus and His followers
Came in and took their seats.
Martha joined them. Mary sat
Right at the Master's feet.

They listened to His wise words.
The minutes passed so fast.
Then Martha thought, *How rude of me.*
I should feed my guests.

She would have stayed to hear much more;
Each word she knew was good.
But she thought about the coming meal.
What could she serve for food?

As her company sat quietly,
Martha left the room to serve.
But Mary stayed at Jesus' feet.
Martha mumbled, "Oh, what nerve!

"She knows that all our visitors
Will be hungry very soon.
Yet there she sits while I prepare
The food out here alone."

The more she worked, the more she thought
About the idle girl.
It's not fair. She sits while I work.
Martha's mind, full of anger, whirled.

Finally, Martha could take no more.
She walked to Jesus' place.
He ceased to speak and looked at her.
She had something to state.

"Excuse me, Master," Martha said aloud.
"Please tell me, don't You care?
I'm working hard to serve some food
While Mary just sits there."

Jesus listened to Martha's words
And then looked down at Mary.
Both were faithful followers.
Both sisters He loved dearly.

"Now, Martha, you are quite the cook.
You want to please; that's true.
You keep house well, and I know
It's important to you too.

"But I am here to tell you things.
I have so much to teach.
Dinner can wait for everyone.
Think not of what to eat.

"Martha, you're a great hostess.
Your talents are unique.
But Mary has chosen to sit right here
And to listen at My feet.

"Don't be distracted by the things
That to the world are a bother.
Don't worry or be troubled.
Just hear the Word of My Father.

"To everything a season comes;
There's a time to sit and hear.
I bring you promises of life—
Of things God holds so dear."

Dear Parents:

The story of Mary and Martha offers several lessons for the Christian family. First, Mary and Martha "opened" their home to Jesus (see Luke 10:38). They welcomed their Lord and Savior and made Him a part of their family life. With your child, identify ways your family has welcomed Jesus. Count the number of crosses and pictures of Jesus in your home. If your child's room does not have a cross or picture of Jesus, purchase or make one together.

Second, this story teaches us about what Jesus thinks is important. While it's important to help one another, it's most important to hear God's Word and learn about Jesus' saving action for us on the cross. Then our actions for one another will grow from the love God has for us.

If you do not already have one, begin a family devotion time. Spend time each day reading God's Word together, either from a children's Bible or a favorite Bible storybook. Pray together often, asking God to strengthen your faith and to help you treat one another with love and respect.

The Editor